O Stacey,

We have been Best Friends for a few great years now. I hope many more to come. Happy Birthday.

I Love You

Beth

Many Strong and Beautiful Women

Reflections on Sisterhood and Friendship

Featuring the artwork of
Kiki Oberstenfeld de Suarez

Kiki

Edited by Jill Wolf

Antioch Publishing Company
Yellow Springs, Ohio 45387

I TAKE CARE OF THE SUN

CONTENTS

☀ SISTERHOOD ☀

Sisterhood—that is, primary and bonding love from women—is, like motherhood, a capacity, not a destiny. It must be chosen, exercised by acts of will.

—Olga Broumas

The love expressed between women is particular and powerful, because we have had to love in order to live; love has been our survival.

—Audre Lorde

I sought my soul,
But my soul I could not see.
I sought my God,
But my God eluded me.
I sought my sisters,
And I found all three.

—Anonymous

All women have a sacred obligation
to each other irrespective of class or
conditions of work.
—Vida Goldstein

I must speak for the women.
—Lucy Stone

Sisters are our peers,
the voice of our times.
—Elizabeth Fishel

The bond between women is a circle
—we are together within it.

—*Judy Grahn*

So closely interwoven have been our
lives, our purposes, and experiences
that, separated, we have a feeling of
incompleteness—united, such strength of
self-assertion that no ordinary obstacles,
differences, or dangers ever appear to
us insurmountable.

—*Elizabeth Cady Stanton*

Sisterhood is powerful.

—*Robin Morgan*

WOMEN MAKE THE WORLD GO 'ROUND

What is done or learned by one class of women, becomes, by virtue of their common womanhood, the property of all women.

—*Elizabeth and Emily Blackwell*

Women's work is always toward wholeness.

—*May Sarton*

For is it not true that human progress is but a mighty growing pattern woven together by the tenuous single threads united in a common effort?

—*Soong Mei-ling (Madame Chiang Kai-shek)*

Ah, my sisters . . . shall we not be able to see those others of our sex who are suffering? Even if we are happy, shall we not have pity on the unhappy ones? A woman need not have endured any wrong herself to feel the wrongs of others.

—*Lillie Devereux Blake*

For when three sisters love each other with such sincere affection, the one does not experience sorrow, pain, or affliction of any kind, but the others' heart wishes to relieve, and vibrates in tenderness.

—*Elizabeth Shaw*

It is only the women whose eyes have been washed clear with tears who get the broad vision that makes them little sisters to all the world.

—*Dorothy Dix*

We are women of different ages, beliefs and lifestyles.

We are women of many economic, social, political, racial, ethnic, cultural, educational and religious backgrounds.

We are married, single, widowed and divorced.

We are mothers and daughters.

We are sisters.

—Declaration of American Women

WOMEN'S SOLIDARITY

Harmony exists in difference no less than in likeness . . . .
                                        —*Margaret Fuller*

A sister can be seen as someone who is both ourselves and very much not ourselves—a special kind of double.
                                        —*Toni McNaron*

A sister is both your mirror—and your opposite.
                                        —*Elizabeth Fishel*

Are we not like the two volumes of one book?
                                        —*Marceline Desbordes-Valmore,*
                                        to her friend Pauline Duchambge

♡ FRIENDSHIP ♡

In thee my soul shall own combined
The sister and the friend.
—Catherine Killigrew

We have been friends together,
In sunshine and in shade . . . .
—Caroline Norton

Those years with Winifred taught
me that the type of friendship
which reaches its apotheosis in
the story of David and Jonathan
is not a monopoly of the masculine
sex. Hitherto, perhaps owing to a
lack of women recorders, this fact
has been found difficult to accept
by men, and even by other women.
—Vera Brittain

I think we owe our friends more,
especially our female friends.
                              —*Fay Weldon*

If we build on a sure foundation in
friendship, we must love our friends
for their sakes rather than for our own.
                              —*Charlotte Brontë*

Friendship with oneself is all-important
because without it one cannot be friends
with anyone else in the world.
                              —*Eleanor Roosevelt*

I have found companions in my female
friends . . . .
                              —*Margherita Datini*

MY DEAREST FRIENDS!

The truth is, friendship is to me every bit as sacred and eternal as marriage.
—Katherine Mansfield

Though Love be deeper, Friendship is more wide . . . .
—Corinne Roosevelt Robinson

Love is like the wild rose-briar;
Friendship like the holly tree.
The holly is dark when the rose-briar blooms,
But which will bloom most constantly?
—Emily Brontë

The only rose without thorns is friendship.
—Magdeleine de Scudéry

Two may talk together under the same roof for many years, yet never really meet; and two others at first speech are old friends.

—*Mary Catherwood*

There was a definite process by which one made people into friends, and it involved talking to them and listening to them for hours at a time.

—*Rebecca West*

Intimacies between women often go backwards, beginning in revelations and ending in small talk without loss of esteem.

—*Elizabeth Bowen*

THE EMBRAC

The only thing to do is to hug one's
friends tight and do one's job.
—Edith Wharton

For Memory has painted this perfect day
With colors that never fade,
And we find at the end of a perfect day
The soul of a friend we've made.
—Carrie Jacobs Bond

You meet your friend, your face
brightens—you have struck gold.
—Kassia

I have long seen "friend" in your mind, in your words, in your actions, but *now* distinctly visible, and clearly written in characters that cannot be distrusted, I discern *true* friend!
—Charlotte Brontë, in a letter to Ellen Nussey

Always a drive to Silchester, or ramble through the woods, was to me joy and delight, health, freedom and happiness; and since I have learnt to think of it as a link in the chain of our friendship, I have loved it more and more.
—Mary Russell Mitford,
in a letter to Elizabeth Barrett Browning

This is the world of light and speech, and I shall take leave to tell you that you are very dear.
—George Eliot (Marian Evans Cross),
in a letter to Mrs. Burne-Jones

I have never been rich before,
But you have poured
Into my heart's high door
A golden hoard.

My wealth is the vision shared,
The sympathy,
The feast of the soul prepared
By you for me.

Together we wander through
The wooded ways.
Old beauties are green and new
Seen through your gaze.

—Anne Campbell

My only sketch, profile, of Heaven is a
large blue sky, and larger than the biggest
I have seen in June—and in it are my
friends—every one of them.

—Emily Dickinson

Many kinds of fruit grow upon the tree
of life, but none so sweet as friendship;
as with the orange tree its blossoms and
fruit appear at the same time, full of
refreshment for sense and for soul.

—Lucy Larcom

Best friend, my well-spring in the
wilderness!

—George Eliot (Marian Evans Cross)

But every road is rough to me
That has no friend to cheer it.

—Elizabeth Shane

GIRLFRIENDS

The odd thing about these deep and
personal connections of women is that they
often ignore barriers of age, economics,
worldly experience, race, culture—all barriers
that, in male or mixed society, had seemed
so difficult to cross.

—*Gloria Steinem*

It is such a comfort to have a friend near.
—Opal Whiteley

The balm of life, a kind and faithful
friend.
—Mercy Otis Warren

Whenever I forget to notice any kindness
of yours, do believe, my beloved friend,
that I have, notwithstanding, marked the
date of it with a white stone, and also
with a heart *not* of stone . . . .
—Elizabeth Barrett Browning,
in a letter to Mary Russell Mitford

With me her generosity and forbearance
were unfailing; patiently she consoled my
lunatic anxiety over adverse reviews,
rejected manuscripts, family ailments, and
other minor everyday annoyances which
to her must have seemed absurdly trivial.
—Vera Brittain, about her friend Winifred Holtby

Always I have a chair for you in the smallest parlor in the world, to wit, my heart.
—*Emily Dickinson*

Friend, what years could us divide?
—*Dinah Maria Mulock Craik*

Perhaps the most delightful friendships are those in which there is much agreement, much disputation, and yet more personal liking.
—*George Eliot (Marian Evans Cross)*

Friendship [is] the unison of well-tuned hearts . . . .
—*Katherine Fowler Philips*

BOOK-WOMAN

. . . that perfect tranquility of life, which is nowhere to be found but in retreat, a faithful friend, and a good library . . . .
—Aphra Behn

There are friends who act as "solvents" in our minds. They help us blend the stiff incongruities of experience into something that will not clog our brains. Our ideas flow more easily when they are around.
—Frances Lester Warner

To have a friend is to have one of the sweetest gifts that life can bring; to be a friend is to have a solemn and tender education of soul from day to day.
—Amy Robertson Brown

Each friend represents a world in us, a world possibly not born until they arrive, and it is only by this meeting that a new world is born.
—Anaïs Nin

SUPPORT AND UNDERSTANDING

For there is no friend like a sister
In calm or stormy weather;
To cheer one on the tedious way,
To fetch one if one goes astray,
To lift one if one totters down,
To strengthen whilst one stands.

—*Christina Rossetti*

They might not need me; but they might.
I'll let my head be just in sight;
A smile as small as mine might be
Precisely their necessity.

—*Emily Dickinson*

I am not afraid to trust my sisters—not I.

—Angelina Grimké

I shall never consent to have our sex
considered in an inferior point of light.

—Abigail Adams

First, no woman should say, "I am but
a woman!" But a woman! What more
could you ask to be?

—Maria Mitchell

We must have perseverance and above all
confidence in ourselves. We must believe
that we are gifted for something . . . .

—Marie Curie

Blessed is the influence of one true,
loving human soul on another.
    —*George Eliot (Marian Evans Cross)*

Two persons love in one another the
future good which they aid one another
to unfold.
    —*Margaret Fuller*

We older women . . . can offer our
younger sisters, at the very least, an
honest report of what we have learned
and how we have grown.
    —*Elizabeth Janeway*

Little deeds of kindness,
  little words of love,
Help to make earth happy
  like the heaven above.
    —*Julia Fletcher Carney*

MOMMY, HELP ME TOUCH THE STARS

Surely we ought to prize those friends on whose principles and opinions we may constantly rely—of whom we may say in all emergencies, "I know what they would think."

—Hannah Farnham Lee

Oh, the comfort, the inexpressible comfort of feeling safe with a person, having neither to weigh thoughts nor measure words, but pouring them all right out, just as they are, chaff and grain together; certain that a faithful hand will take and sift them, keep what is worth keeping, and then with the breath of kindness blow the rest away.

—Dinah Maria Mulock Craik

Even though I can't solve your problems, I will be there as your sounding board whenever you need me.

—Sandra K. Lamberson

Since she was my sister and we did the same work, I could say things to her that I couldn't say to anyone else.
—*Catherine Deneuve*

Neither of us had ever known any pleasure quite equal to the joy of coming home at the end of the day after a series of separate and varied experiences, and each recounting these incidents to the other over late biscuits and tea.
—*Vera Brittain*

Guard within yourself that treasure, kindness. Know how to give without hesitation, how to lose without regret, how to acquire without meanness. Know how to replace in your heart, by the happiness of those you love, the happiness that may be wanting to yourself.
—*George Sand (Amandine Dupin)*

WOMEN HELP WOMEN

Help one another, is part of the religion
of our sisterhood, Fan.

—Louisa May Alcott

Those whom we support hold us up
in life.

—Marie Ebner von Eschenbach

I've always believed that one woman's
success can only help another woman's
success.

—Gloria Vanderbilt

Sisters stand between one and life's
cruel circumstances.

—Nancy Milford

Female friendships that work are
relationships in which women help
each other to belong to themselves.

—Louise Bernikow

I like to help women help themselves . . . .

—Louisa May Alcott

What do we live for, if it is not to make life less difficult to each other?
—*George Eliot (Marian Evans Cross)*

Sometimes, sisters have the same journey in their hearts. One may help the other or betray her.
—*Louise Bernikow*

. . . as nobody can do more mischief to a woman than a woman, so perhaps might one reverse the maxim and say nobody can do more good.
—*Elizabeth Holland*

I used to be awfully proud of her being my sister. I don't know what I would have done without her.
—*Jessamyn West*

🐦 GENERATIONS 🐦

So many things we love are you, I can't
seem to explain except by little things, but
flowers and beautiful handmade things—
small stitches. So much of our reading and
thinking—so many sweet customs and so
much of our . . . well, our religion. It is
all *you*. I hadn't realized it before. This is
so vague but do you see a little, dear
Grandma? I want to thank you.
                              —*Anne Morrow Lindbergh*

We are together, my child and I. Mother
and child, yes, but *sisters* really, against
whatever denies us all that we are.
                              —*Alice Walker*

Mummy herself has told us that she looked upon us more as her friends than her daughters.

—Anne Frank

The grandchildren were always delighted to see her . . . . They enjoyed her because she obviously enjoyed them.

—Peregrine Churchill

You come from a tribe of feisty foremothers. It's up to you to walk in their footsteps and continue their journey.

—Letty Cottin Pogrebin

WOMEN FLOATING HAPPILY IN THE FLOW OF LIFE

One sister have I in our house,
And one, a hedge away.
There's only one recorded,
But both belong to me.
                    —*Emily Dickinson,*
        about her sister and sister-in-law

My home is humble and unattractive
to strangers, but to me it contains what
I shall find nowhere else in the world
—the profound, the intense affection
which brothers and sisters feel for each
other when their minds are cast in the
same mould, their ideas drawn from the
same source—when they have clung to
each other from childhood, and when
disputes have never sprung up to divide
them.
                              —*Charlotte Brontë*

Whatever the author's intentions, the
heroine was my sister.

—*Mavis Gallant*

My sister! With that thrilling word
Let thoughts unnumbered wildly spring!
What echoes in my heart are stirred,
While thus I touch the trembling string.

—*Margaret Davidson*

. . . I cannot deny that, now I am
without your company I feel not only
that I am deprived of a very dear sister,
but that I have lost half of myself.

—*Beatrice d'Este, in a letter to her sister*

EVERY MOTHER IS A HARDWORKING WOMA.

Four sisters, parted for an hour,
None lost, one only gone before,
Made by love's immortal power,
Nearest and dearest evermore.
Oh, when these hidden stores of ours
Lie open to the Father's sight,
May they be rich in golden hours,
Deeds that show fairer for the light,
Lives whose brave music long shall ring,
Like a spirit-stirring strain,
Souls that shall gladly soar and sing
In the long sunshine after rain.

—Louisa May Alcott

About the Artist—

Kiki Oberstenfeld de Suarez lives and paints in the beautiful highlands of Chiapas in southern Mexico. She is German by birth and upbringing, and a psychologist by education. More than ten years ago, chance brought her to the little colonial town of San Cristobal de las Casas, where she fell in love, started a family, and began to paint.

Kiki's paintings reflect the bold colors of the Mexican landscape and the vibrant culture of her adopted homeland. The images she chooses to paint express her belief in the good things of life —love, peace, friendship, fellowship, and a deep appreciation of nature and the wholeness of everything on earth. Her style is simple, honest, and personal, yet it is also universal, for it illustrates important values shared by people everywhere.

In just a few short years Kiki's fame has grown from a small grass roots movement to worldwide recognition. Kiki is the author and illustrator of three children's books and her paintings, cards, T-shirts, posters, and other licensed products are in great demand.